GROUNDBREAKERS

Sieur de La Salle

Andrew Santella

Heinemann Library
Chicago, Illinois

© 2002 Reed Educational & Professional Publishing
Published by Heinemann Library,
an imprint of Reed Educational & Professional Publishing,
Chicago, Illinois

Customer Service 888-454-2279

Visit our website at www.heinemannlibrary.com

Design and maps by Wilkinson Design
Printed and bound in the U.S.A. by Lake Book Manufacturing, Inc.

06 05 04 03 02
10 9 8 7 6 5 4 3 2 1

Library of Congress Cataloging-in-Publication Data
Santella, Andrew.
    Sieur de La Salle / Andrew Santella.
      p. cm. — (Groundbreakers)
    Includes bibliographical references and index.
    Summary: Presents an account of LaSalle's life and explorations and
    examines their impact on history and the world.
      ISBN 1-58810-598-9
      1. La Salle, Robert Cavelier, sieur de, 1643-1687—Juvenile
    literature. 2. Explorers—North America—Biography—Juvenile
    literature. 3. Explorers—France—Biography—Juvenile literature. 4.
    North America—Discovery and exploration—French—Juvenile literature.
    5. Mississippi River Valley—Discovery and
    exploration—French—Juvenile literature. 6. Mississippi River
    Valley—History—To 1803—Juvenile literature. [1. La Salle, Robert
    Cavelier, sieur de, 1643-1687. 2. Explorers. 3. Mississippi
    River—Discovery and exploration.] I. Title. II. Series.
      F1030.5 .S26 2002
      977'.01'092—dc21
                                        2001004033

Acknowledgments
The author and publishers are grateful to the following for permission to reproduce copyright material:
pp. 4, 18, 19, 20, 21, 22, 26, 31, 32, 36, 39 North Wind Picture Archives; p. 5 Nathan Benn/Corbis; p. 6
Vanni Archive/Corbis; p. 7 Eye Ubiquitous/Corbis; pp. 8, 24 Corbis; p. 9 Hulton/Archive by Getty Images;
p. 10 Stock Montage; p. 11 The Newberry Library, Chicago; pp. 12, 14, 16 The Granger Collection, New
York; p. 13 Robert Estall/Corbis; pp. 15, 30, 34 Bettman/Corbis; p. 17 Dallas and John Heaton/Corbis; p.
23 Paul A. Souders/Corbis; p. 25 Courtesy of the University of Central Arkansas Archives and the
Arkansas State History Commission; p. 28 Robert Lifson/Heinemann Library; p. 29 Richard Hamilton
Smith/Corbis; p. 33 David Muench/Corbis; p. 37 Texas Historical Commission; p. 38 Robert
Clark/Aurora/PictureQuest; p. 40 Anna Mycek-Wodecki.

Cover photograph courtesy of North Wind Picture Archives.

Some words are shown in bold, **like this.** You can find
out what they mean by looking in the glossary.

Contents

Who Was La Salle?

In 1666, a Frenchman arrived in Montréal, which was then just a small **frontier** village at the western edge of the French territory in North America. His name was René-Robert Cavelier, Sieur de La Salle, and his ambitions were as grand as his name.

La Salle's plan

By 1666, the powerful nations of Europe had already claimed much of North America as their own. Spain had built large cities in Mexico. The English ran thriving **colonies** in Virginia and New England. French traders pushed deep into the rugged wilderness they called New France, or Canada.

For 21 years after coming to Montréal, La Salle worked tirelessly to extend France's possessions in North America. He explored places no European had ever seen. He became the first European to travel down the Mississippi River all the way to the Gulf of Mexico. He built forts along the Great Lakes and the rivers in the middle of North America. He dreamed that these forts would be the foundation of rich French **empire** based on trading furs and other natural **resources** of North America. His efforts to build that empire eventually cost him his life.

La Salle's plans led him deep into the interior of North America.

The Mississippi River flows from Minnesota to the Gulf of Mexico. La Salle was the first European to travel down the river to its mouth.

La Salle and his followers

La Salle won the support of France's most important people, including King Louis XIV. One of La Salle's followers called him "one of the greatest men of this age." However, he also made many enemies, including some of the men he commanded. On several occasions, men under La Salle's command deserted him. Three different times, men under his command tried to kill him. In 1687, they finally succeeded.

What was it about La Salle that provoked such hatred? Much of what we know about La Salle comes from journals and other records kept by the people who traveled with him. Very little of La Salle's own writing has survived. Some of his men said he was too cruel to his followers. With La Salle, one wrote, "pleasure was often **banished.**" Also, he led his men into dangerous situations in unknown territories. Understandably, they were sometimes afraid to go on. La Salle seems to have lacked the ability to convince them of the importance of their work.

La Salle himself never seemed to lack courage. When accidents or bad weather or bad luck upset his plans, La Salle simply pushed on and tried again. From the icy St. Lawrence River to the hot Gulf of Mexico, La Salle never stopped trying to build his French empire in North America.

Education of an Explorer

La Salle was born in 1643, near the French city of Rouen. No one is certain of the date of his birth. However, records show that he was **baptized** in the Roman Catholic Church in Rouen on November 22, 1643. On the baptismal record, he is called simply Robert Cavelier.

Rouen's Catholic cathedral is famous for its beautiful stained glass windows.

In the words of one of La Salle's teachers:

"He is a restless boy."

The Cavelier family

The Caveliers were one of the largest and richest families in Rouen. Robert's father was a cloth merchant who was wealthy enough to own a large **estate** near Rouen. Robert may have been born on this estate, which was called La Salle. By the time he was an adult, Robert was known as "Sieur de La Salle," which means "the gentleman from La Salle." This was a typical way for wealthy people of the time to identify themselves.

Rouen is on the Seine River, about halfway between Paris and the English Channel. In La Salle's time, it was a center of the cloth trade. Weavers in Rouen made linen that was **exported** to French and Spanish **colonies** in North and South America. More than 1,000 trading ships sailed into Rouen's port each year, bound for distant lands.

A Jesuit education

Even as a boy, La Salle began learning about travel to distant lands. He attended a school run by an order of Catholic priests called **Jesuits.** The order was founded in 1540 and was dedicated to spreading the Catholic faith all over the world.

Rouen's location along the Seine helped make it a thriving port city.

When La Salle was a boy, Jesuit priests were at work in North America, South America, Japan, India, and Africa. In France's colony in North America, Jesuits pushed far into the unmapped wilderness to teach the Native Americans about Christianity. Jesuits wrote about their travels, and these writings were part of La Salle's early education.

It was a very strict education. Students woke before sunrise and kept busy all day long with classes, prayers, studying, and more prayers. La Salle learned Latin, Greek, and the basics of several other languages. He learned all there was to know about **astronomy** and science. Most of all, La Salle learned mathematics. Math skills were essential for mapmakers, and the Jesuits were pioneers in the new science of **cartography.** La Salle showed so much talent that his superiors began preparing him for the priesthood. However, La Salle had other ideas.

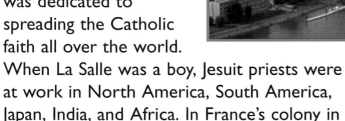

BLACK ROBES

Jesuit **missionaries** worked all over the world to spread Christianity. In Canada, they lived among Native Americans far from European colonies. Native Americans sometimes called Jesuit priests "Black Robes," because they wore their heavy priests' robes even as they paddled canoes and struggled through dense forests. One of the most famous Jesuits in Canada was Father Jacques Marquette. With Louis Jolliet, he led the first expedition by Europeans to travel much of the length of the Mississippi River.

New France

La Salle wanted to travel. In 1666, he asked his superiors to assign him to work in China. When they turned down that request, he asked for a job in Portugal. They turned him down again. Instead, they assigned him to teach grammar in a series of small French towns. This was not the life La Salle had in mind for himself. He resigned the **Jesuit** order and headed out on his own.

The French in Canada

La Salle set his sights on North America. French explorers had been sailing the St. Lawrence River there for over 100 years. They called the area *Le Canada*, based on the Native American word *kanata*, which means "village." After several tries, the French established a successful **colony** along the St. Lawrence.

Mapmakers also called the area "New France."

La Salle's older brother already lived in New France. He was a priest living in Montréal. La Salle had heard about life in Montréal. It was still a small town, with about 200 inhabitants, but it sounded exciting to him. The town was full of activity. Native Americans brought animal furs to Montréal to sell. Explorers and **missionaries** used Montréal as a base for long trips into the wilderness. In the spring of 1666, La Salle decided to go to Montréal and start a new life there.

Crossing the Atlantic Ocean meant spending weeks on board a crowded ship.

8

This illustration shows Québec in 1664, just before La Salle's arrival in New France.

An ocean crossing

Crossing the Atlantic Ocean to New France took anywhere between six and twelve weeks. For travelers like La Salle, these were very long, uncomfortable weeks. Passengers squeezed into cramped quarters below deck, with very little light or fresh air. There was little room for them to stretch out on deck. Coils of rope, chicken coops, and barrels of supplies were scattered everywhere. Most likely, there were even cows on board, making the journey to their new home in New France. Passengers were surely relieved when signs of nearby land began to appear after weeks at sea.

La Salle's ship landed at Québec, the capital of New France. Québec stood atop a **bluff** along the St. Lawrence River and was the home of the colonial governor. Montréal was 150 miles (241 kilometers) further up the St. Lawrence. The only way to get there was on a riverboat. The French had not yet cut roads through the forests.

THE FUR TRADE

The forests and rivers of Canada were ideal homes for beavers. To survive cold Canadian winters, the animals grew thick, glossy coats. These furs from Canada were **exported** to France, where they were made into felt hats and other kinds of clothing. These garments were the height of fashion in France in the 1600s. The demand for beaver **pelts** was so great that fur trappers depleted the number of beavers in many places. To find more, they pushed deeper and deeper into the North American wilderness.

La Salle may have come to Montréal because his older brother was living there. La Salle's brother was named Jean, and he belonged to an order of priests called the Sulpicians. They wanted smart and ambitious young people to join them in Montréal, to help make the city grow. The Sulpicians owned a great deal of land near Montréal, and to attract people, they sold the land at bargain rates. La Salle bought several thousand acres from the priests and began turning it into his home.

Clearing the land

The first challenge was clearing the land. It was overgrown with pine trees that had to be cut down. Then the stumps of the trees had to be either chopped up or burned out. It was very hard work, but soon La Salle had cleared a place for himself. In France, a wealthy person like La Salle probably would have hired someone to do this kind of work. But La Salle was starting a new life in Canada, and it would be very different from his life in Europe. To make money, La Salle divided his land into smaller lots that he rented to other colonists.

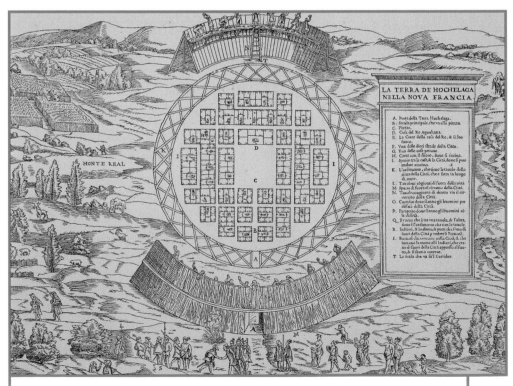

*When La Salle arrived in Montréal, it was still a small **frontier** village.*

The Seneca befriended La Salle and helped him learn their language.

La Salle's land was in the middle of a vast forest. Little by little, he began learning his way around the new land. This was a different kind of education from the one he'd had in France, but it would be just as valuable. He went off on his own for long hikes deep into the woods. He learned to survive alone in the woods in the worst winter weather. He learned that he could make a meal of the ants that he found when he peeled back the bark of some trees. He learned to identify animals by the tracks they made. And he learned that in summer, his worst enemy was the mosquito. They swarmed constantly and the only way to drive them away was to build a smoky fire. Or La Salle might cover his body with bear grease to keep the mosquitoes from landing on him.

Learning the language

La Salle's most important lesson was learning Native American languages. In the fall of 1667, two Seneca came to live on La Salle's land. With their help, he was soon able to speak their language. La Salle must have been already making plans to travel into the interior of Canada. If so, he knew he would need to communicate with the Native Americans there. That winter, his Seneca guests told him something that made him want to begin his journey right away.

News of a Great River

Jacques Cartier led three voyages of exploration in Canada in the 1500s.

The Senceca told La Salle of a "great river" to the south. Follow this river for several months, they told La Salle, and it will carry you all the way to the sea. The Seneca were probably talking about the Ohio and Mississippi Rivers. The Ohio River leads to the Mississippi River, which flows into the Gulf of Mexico.

Searching for a route to Asia

What the Seneca told him about the river set La Salle's mind racing. To understand why, it helps to remember what drew many Europeans to North America in the first place. Christopher Columbus was searching for a sea route to Asia when he arrived in 1492. Europeans wanted to get to Asia to trade for spices and other valuable goods. Even after Columbus, explorers continued to look for a route to Asia. France sent Jacques Cartier to look in 1531. He mapped parts of what became Canada, but never found such a route. As other explorers learned the vastness of North America, hope for a shortcut to Asia faded.

JACQUES CARTIER

Jacques Cartier (1491–1557) was the discoverer of the St. Lawrence River. He sailed from France to Canada three times, traveling as far west as the future site of Montréal. To get a view of the surrounding countryside, he climbed a mountain there that he named Mont Réal. Montréal was later named for that mountain. La Salle made Montréal his home 130 years later.

Instead, they found something just as valuable. North America was full of natural **resources,** like furs—and fortunes could be made selling them to Europe. But this required fast and reliable means of transportation. There were no roads through the wilderness. Lakes and rivers were the highways of the time. The St. Lawrence River was one such trade route. La Salle's "great river" could be another one. La Salle had no idea if the river led to a shortcut to Asia. But he knew for sure that it could help transport the valuable trade goods of North America. That was why he was so eager to find it.

Forts for the French

He imagined building a string of French forts along the river. He would make allies of the native Americans who lived nearby and they would bring their trade goods to the forts to sell to the French. Soon, French settlers would follow. They would help farm the land and harvest its great forests. French traders would float these goods down the river to the sea, where French ships would wait to take them to Europe. In La Salle's plan, France would control North America's rivers, and therefore would control North America itself. In La Salle's plan, France would grow richer off North America's resources. In the spring of 1669, he set to work turning his plan into reality.

The St. Lawrence River was an important route to the interior of North America.

La Salle's First Exploration

YOU CAN
FOLLOW
LA SALLE'S
JOURNEY
ON THE
MAP ON
PAGES
42–43.

La Salle began organizing an expedition to look for the Mississippi River. First he traveled by canoe back to Québec to tell the French governor, the Marquis de Courcelles, about his plans. Courcelles liked La Salle's plan, but he urged La Salle to travel with a group of French **missionary** priests heading in the same direction. La Salle didn't like the idea of traveling with the priests, but he had little choice. He sold his property to pay for supplies and to hire twelve men of his own. Then, on July 6, 1669, La Salle and 23 other men set off from Montréal in 7 canoes.

River travel

They headed west up the St. Lawrence River, against a rushing current. In many places, large boulders or waterfalls or other obstacles blocked the way of the canoes. When this happened, the travelers had to paddle ashore, pick up their canoes, and carry them overland around the obstacles. Only then could they resume paddling upstream. These short walks could be exhausting.

Native Americans made lightweight, sturdy canoes on wood frames covered in strips of bark from the birch tree.

14

The men had to carry heavy loads on their back. Mosquitoes buzzed around their heads, tormenting them. Often there was nowhere to walk except on slippery rocks in shallow water or through dense bushes.

Because they had to carry their canoes over land, travelers learned to make light but sturdy canoes, much like the ones the Native Americans had long used. The frames of these canoes were made from the wood of cedar trees. Over this frame were laid strips of bark from birch trees. Some birch-bark canoes were light enough that one man could easily carry one on his back.

An exhausting journey

For weeks, La Salle and the others paddled and walked westward. At night, they were so tired that they fell fast asleep almost as soon as they lay down. One of the priests, Father Galinée, kept a diary of the trip. He wrote, "If the weather is fair, you make a fire and lie down to sleep without further trouble. But if it rains, you must peel bark from the trees, and make a shed by laying it on a frame of sticks."

AN
ACCOUNT
OF
Monfieur *de la* SALLE's
LAST
Expedition and DISCOVERIES
IN
North *AMERICA.*
Prefented to the *French* King,

And Publifhed by the

Chevalier *Tonti*, Governour of Fort St. *Louis*, in the Province of the *Iflinois.*

Made *Englifh* from the *Paris* Original.

ALSO
The ADVENTURES of the Sieur· *de MONTAUBAN*, Captain of the French Buccaneers on the Coaft of *Guinea*, in the Year 1695.

LONDON
Printed for *J. Tonfon* at the *Judge's Head*, and *S. Buckley* at the *Dolphin* in *Fleet-ftreet*, and *R. Knaplock*, at the *Angel* and *Grown* in St. *Paul's Church-Yard.* 1698.

Journals and reports of explorations in the New World were popular with readers in Europe, and stories of La Salle's trip sold well.

Almost one month after leaving Montréal, La Salle and the others arrived at Lake Ontario. The lake was larger than they had expected. Galinée wrote that it was "like a great sea with no land beyond it." There were more surprises ahead.

Into the Unknown

You can follow La Salle's journey on the map on pages 42–43.

La Salle and the others stayed close to the shore of Lake Ontario and paddled to the west. Near the site of present-day Rochester, New York, they came upon a group of Seneca. The Seneca invited the French to follow them to their village. La Salle and nine others decided to go with the Seneca, walking for several hours to reach the village. The Seneca village was on a hill, surrounded by a fence of wooden stakes, or **palisades.** Inside the fence were lodges with walls made of birch-bark—the same material the Native Americans and French used for their canoes.

With the Seneca

La Salle and the other Frenchmen stayed with the Seneca for weeks. The two groups got along well at first. They exchanged gifts and shared feasts of dog meat and roasted bear claws. However, relations between the French and Seneca soon worsened. The Seneca began to frighten the French. One day, the Seneca captured a Native American from another village after a small battle. The Seneca invited the La Salle and the other Frenchmen to watch as they tortured and then killed their prisoner. La Salle knew that Native American tribes of the area practiced torture. For that matter, so did some Europeans. However, this was probably the first time he had seen the practice up close. Not surprisingly, he and his fellow travelers wasted no time leaving the Seneca village. Soon they were back on Lake Ontario, paddling west.

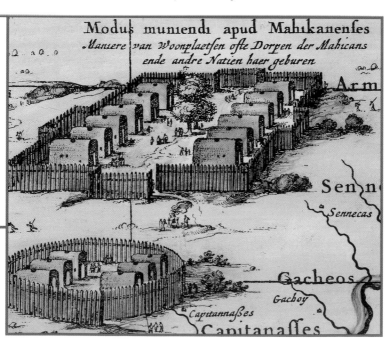

Some Native American villages were protected by fences made of wooden stakes.

The Niagara Falls are beautiful to look at, but river travelers like La Salle saw them as a dangerous obstacle.

Niagara Falls

They soon passed the mouth of a large river. They could hear the crashing and roaring of a waterfall in the distance. They were at the Niagara River, and the roaring they heard came from the Niagara Falls. The falls would later become a popular tourist destination, but La Salle and the priests did not stop to admire the scene. To them, the Niagara River appeared to be full of **hazards.**

NIKA

One of La Salle's guides on his first expedition was a Shawnee named Nika. He became one of La Salle's most trusted companions. He later traveled to France with La Salle and was with the explorer on his final voyage.

Instead, the group continued across Lake Ontario. When they reached the western end of the lake, they paused to decide their next move. The priests wanted to continue west along the connected Great Lakes. They hoped to build **missions** along the shores of Lake Superior, far to the northwest, and preach to the Native Americans there. La Salle had other plans. He saw this as his opportunity to split off from the priests and begin his own exploration to the south.

17

The Mysterious Journey

YOU CAN FOLLOW LA SALLE'S JOURNEY ON THE MAP ON PAGES 42–43.

La Salle told Father Galinée and the others that he was too ill to continue traveling and that he planned to return to Montréal. The priests blessed La Salle, wished him a safe journey home, and pushed on to the west. Only after the priests were gone did La Salle reveal his true plans to the thirteen men who stayed with him. They weren't returning to Montréal at all, but rather, they were going in search of the rivers that led to the sea.

La Salle's lost journal

La Salle had not wanted to travel with the priests in the first place, so now he was glad to be in command of his own expedition. He could plot his own travels without having to consult anyone else. Unfortunately, no one is sure exactly where La Salle went after he left the priests. Father Galinée and the other priests were trained to keep careful records of their travels and had been educated to draw accurate maps. That is how we know all the details of La Salle's trip down the St. Lawrence River and across Lake Ontario. However, La Salle's activities after he left the priests remain largely a mystery. If La Salle kept a record of his travels, that record has disappeared. Ever since then, historians have debated about where La Salle went and what La Salle did from 1669 to 1671.

La Salle may have traveled down the Ohio River as far as the site of present-day Louisville, Kentucky, but he turned back before reaching the Mississippi River.

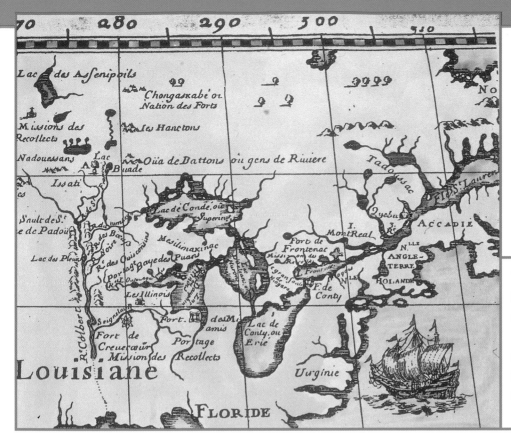

This map of the Great Lakes region from the 1600s was based on the travels of French explorers.

The Ohio River

It seems likely that La Salle and his men headed south from Lake Ontario. With help from Indian guides, they may have made their way to the Ohio River. They may have been the first Europeans to see the Ohio River. According to one account, La Salle reached "a place where the river drops from a great height into a vast **marshland,** below the point where it is joined by a very large river flowing from the north." Some historians think that this is a description of the site now occupied by the city of Louisville, Kentucky. Others are not sure that La Salle traveled that far west. Most agree, however, that at some point his men abandoned him. Alone, or maybe with a few Native American guides, he probably explored the area between the Ohio River and the Great Lakes.

No one is sure what La Salle saw on his long, solitary journey. However, he would soon have proof that the Ohio and Mississippi rivers could be followed to the Gulf of Mexico.

Building Fort Frontenac

YOU CAN FOLLOW LA SALLE'S JOURNEY ON THE MAP ON PAGES 42–43.

Somehow La Salle made his way back to Montréal. His arrival there in 1671 surprised the residents of the village, who had already given him up for dead. Others feared that La Salle had lost his mind in the wilderness. His men had abandoned him and now the residents of Montréal talked about him behind his back. However, one very important person befriended La Salle and supported his plans. His name was Louis de Buade, the Count of Frontenac. In 1672, Frontenac became governor of New France.

Working with Frontenac

La Salle and Frontenac had long talks about La Salle's plans to build French forts and trading posts along the waterways of North America. The governor agreed to help make La Salle's plan a reality. They planned to build the first fort on the eastern shore of Lake Ontario, where the St. Lawrence River begins. Their first task was to win the trust of the Iroquois **Confederacy.** This was a powerful group of five Native American tribes that controlled huge stretches of land south of the St. Lawrence River. The Iroquois sometimes attacked French settlements and French **missionaries.** La Salle and Frontenac wanted to be sure that their forts would be safe from Iroquois attacks.

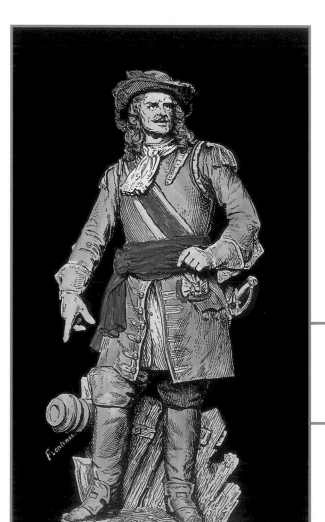

The Count of Frontenac believed that France should expand its North American possessions to the west.

20

A great meeting

In the spring of 1673, La Salle traveled to the Iroquois villages and met with their leaders. He asked them to gather on the shores of Lake Ontario for a meeting with Frontenac. To impress the Native Americans, Frontenac arrived dressed in the full costume of a European **nobleman.** A fleet of hundreds of canoes and **flatboats** accompanied him.

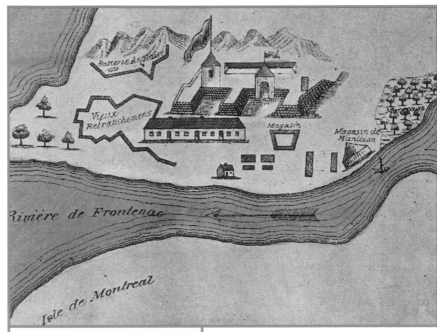

This illustration shows the layout of Fort Frontenac.

Frontenac assured the Iroquois that his intentions were peaceful, and he showered them with gifts. He handed out biscuits, wine, brandy, fresh fruit, heavy coats, and even marbles. When all the speeches were concluded and the gifts were distributed, Frontenac and La Salle got what they came for. The Iroquois agreed to allow the French to build a fort on the shore of Lake Ontario. It would be called Fort Frontenac. It was the first step in La Salle's plans for New France.

MARQUETTE AND JOLLIET

La Salle wasn't the only explorer that Governor Frontenac supported. In 1673, he sent Louis Jolliet and Father Jacques Marquette to look for the Mississippi River. They canoed down the river from present-day Wisconsin to the Arkansas River. They did no go any further because they were worried that Spanish settlers at the mouth of the river would attack them. However, their discoveries confirmed La Salle's belief that the Mississippi River led to the Gulf of Mexico. Unfortunately, Jolliet's canoe overturned on the return trip, and his maps and journals were lost, although he survived.

Return to France

In 1674, La Salle sailed back to France to meet with advisers to King Louis XIV and win support for his plans. La Salle spent the winter of 1674–1675 in France. By now, La Salle was probably more comfortable in the backwoods of New France than in the royal palace, with all its fancy gardens and beautiful works of art. Still, he made valuable **allies** there. He brought with him a letter of recommendation from Governor Frontenac that called La Salle "a man of intelligence and ability." La Salle became friends with Jean-Baptiste Colbert, one of the king's most trusted advisers. With Colbert's help, La Salle was given permission to take charge of Fort Frontenac.

THE SUN KING

King Louis XIV of France, who ruled from 1643 to 1715, was sometimes called "The Sun King," because he was supposed to be the most brilliant ruler in the world. During his long reign, he had great influence over French arts and culture. However, his expensive tastes and the wars he fought with other nations left his country deep in debt. At the time of La Salle's visits in 1674 and 1677, the King was overseeing construction of a new palace. Located in the village of Versailles, the palace was completed in 1682, and it still attracts visitors from all over the world.

A booming business

Returning to New France, La Salle began improving Fort Frontenac. He was soon running a fabulously successful fur trade. Fort Frontenac had several advantages over Montréal in the competition for trade. The fort was more conveniently located for Native Americans near the Great Lakes. Besides, beavers and other animals were still plentiful near the Great Lakes. Along the St. Lawrence River near Montréal, the animals were already becoming harder to find.

Furs from beavers and other animals could bring a fortune for French traders in the 1600s.

Friends and enemies

In fact, La Salle's Fort Frontenac was so successful that traders in Montréal became jealous. They even tried to poison him once. La Salle was not frightened off, however. By 1677, he was ready to return to France again. This time, he wanted to ask the king's permission to build more forts. He explained to the king's advisers that the forts would stretch all along the Great Lakes and the Mississippi River. He told them that the forts would give France control of North America and its valuable **resources.** La Salle must have been very convincing. In a letter addressed to "our dear and beloved Robert Cavelier, Sieur de La Salle," King Louis wrote that La Salle could "build forts at such places as you may think necessary." La Salle had the permission he needed.

Building the *Griffon*

YOU CAN
FOLLOW
LA SALLE'S
JOURNEY
ON THE
MAP ON
PAGES
42–43.

Besides winning the king's favor, La Salle also made a friend in France. His name was Henri de Tonti. Born in Italy, Tonti had moved to France and become an officer in the French army. By the time he met La Salle, Tonti had lost one hand in battle. In its place, doctors had given him an artificial hand. La Salle was so impressed with Tonti that he convinced the Italian to join him in New France. Tonti became La Salle's most trusted officer. On July 14, 1678, La Salle and Tonti set sail for New France. They took with them 30 other men, including carpenters, **blacksmiths,** and other craftsmen. La Salle would need their skills at the new forts he planned to build.

A transport ship

Before he started building forts, La Salle started another building project. Upon his arrival in New France, he began building a large sailing ship to cruise up and down the Great Lakes. On a map, it looks like La Salle could simply sail a ship from the ocean, up the St. Lawrence River and into the Great Lakes. However, he knew that near Montréal, the St. Lawrence became too narrow and rocky for large ships. More obstacles lay further west.

The Griffon *was probably the first large sailing ship to sail the Great Lakes.*

24

The biggest obstacle was Niagara Falls, which would destroy any ship. Beyond the falls, though, it was clear sailing. La Salle decided to build a base near Niagara Falls and build his ship there.

From that point, the ship could travel west as far as present-day Duluth, Minnesota, or as far south as present-day Chicago. Then it could return to Niagara Falls loaded with furs—many more furs than could be carried in any canoe. It could also help transport cannons and other supplies to the forts La Salle planned to build.

The launch of the *Griffon*

In the fall of 1678, La Salle's men began working on the ship. It took nearly one year to complete. Finally, on August 7, 1679, La Salle was ready to launch his new ship on Lake Erie. It was 50 feet (15 meters) long and 16 feet (5 meters) wide, with two masts for sails. La Salle named it the *Griffon*. He fired one of the five small cannons on board, ordered the sails unfurled, and soon a strong breeze was pushing the ship westward. With every mile, La Salle felt closer to realizing his dreams.

NAMING THE *GRIFFON*

La Salle's ship was named for a mythological creature called the **griffin,** which was the family symbol of Governor Frontenac. The griffin was supposed to have the head and wings of an eagle, and the body and tail of a lion.

To the Illinois Prairies

YOU CAN
FOLLOW
LA SALLE'S
JOURNEY
ON THE
MAP ON
PAGES
42–43.

Within weeks La Salle and the *Griffon* had reached Green Bay, an **inlet** on the western shore of Lake Michigan. His men traded with the local native Americans and soon had gathered an impressive collection of furs. On September 18, 1679, La Salle sent the furs back toward Fort Frontenac on board the *Griffon*.

Bad news

He and the rest of his men continued south in canoes. The choppy waters of Lake Michigan nearly drowned the explorers, but in November they arrived at the mouth of the St. Joseph River. There, near the southern tip of Lake Michigan, La Salle had his men begin building another fort. He named it Fort Miami, after a nearby Native American tribe. Then some terrible news reached La Salle. The *Griffon* had disappeared, probably wrecked in a storm on Lake Michigan. With the *Griffon* sunk, La Salle lost a fortune in fur trading income. Worse yet, he would not be able to depend on the *Griffon* to send supplies back and forth to his new forts. One of the priests traveling with La Salle wrote that La Salle's misfortunes "would have made anybody but him give up the enterprise." But instead, La Salle pushed on.

To get from one river to another, explorers sometimes portaged, carrying their canoes and supplies with them.

Pushing on

On December 3, 1679, he and a group of men set off for the Mississippi River. First, they paddled up the St. Joseph River. Near the site of South Bend, Indiana, they carried their canoes from the St. Joseph River to the nearby Kankakee River. This was called making a **portage.** Now La Salle was headed in the right direction. The Kankakee led La Salle to the Illinois River. On January 5, 1680, he began building another fort, near the site of present-day Peoria, Illinois. He named it Fort Crèvecoeur, or Fort Heartbreak. However, the worst heartbreaks were still ahead.

A CRUEL COMMANDER?

La Salle almost always had uneasy relations with the men he commanded. During the walk from the St. Joseph River to the Kankakee, one of his men tried to kill La Salle. It would not be the last attempt on his life. La Salle denied that he was cruel to his men. "It will not be found that I have in any case whatever treated any man harshly," he wrote. Still, La Salle grew more distrustful of those around him.

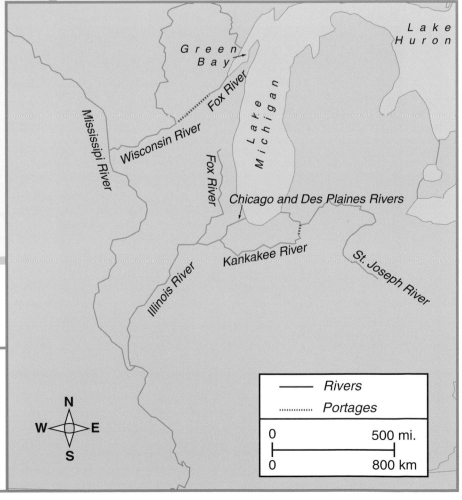

This map shows the system of rivers and lakes that led explorers like La Salle and Marquette and Jolliet to the Mississippi River.

To the Mississippi River

YOU CAN FOLLOW LA SALLE'S JOURNEY ON THE MAP ON PAGES 42–43.

In the spring of 1680, La Salle left Tonti in charge of Fort Crèvecoeur and returned to Montréal to get more supplies. When he reached Fort Frontenac months later, he heard that his men at Fort Crèvecoeur had deserted. They chased Tonti away and destroyed the fort. Then they returned to Fort Miami and did the same thing there. La Salle heard that the traitors were coming to Fort Frontenac to murder him. This advance warning allowed him to surprise the traitors and have them arrested.

Ruined forts

He rushed west to find Tonti and save what he could of his ruined forts. He found Fort Crèvecoeur completely destroyed. The Illinois Indians' village had been destroyed too, by an attack from rival Iroquois. The Iroquois murdered many of the Illinois and left their bodies for La Salle to find.

The only good news was that Tonti was still alive. The two friends were reunited that summer, and they surely talked about the many setbacks La Salle had suffered. He was not yet ready to give up his plan to explore the Mississippi River and build forts there. In the winter of 1681, he assembled a new crew to search for the Mississippi.

La Salle paddled down the Chicago River, where skyscrapers would one day crowd the shore.

When rivers froze over, travelers simply dragged their canoes on sleds over the ice.

La Salle's crew included 23 Frenchmen who were still willing to follow him, including a **gunsmith** and a surgeon. There were also eighteen Native Americans, from Eastern tribes friendly to the French. Some even took their wives and children along. Finally, there was a priest named Zenobe Membré, who kept a journal of the trip.

Reaching the Mississippi

On December 21, 1681, La Salle and his crew set off from Fort Miami. They crossed Lake Michigan and came to the spot that would later be occupied by the skyscrapers of Chicago. It was so cold that many of the rivers were frozen. They placed their canoes on sleds and walked down the frozen waterways. Finally, they reached open water and paddled until they came to the Mississippi River on February 6, 1682. Neither La Salle nor any of his men had ever seen the Mississippi.

Finally, La Salle was on the great river that his Seneca friends had told him about, fifteen years earlier.

PADDLING INSTEAD OF SAILING

La Salle planned to build a second sailing ship like the *Griffon* for the trip down the Mississippi. However, after deciding that it would take too long, he chose to use canoes.

Claiming Louisiana for France

YOU CAN FOLLOW LA SALLE'S JOURNEY ON THE MAP ON PAGES 42–43.

The Mississippi River's gentle current carried La Salle's group steadily southward. At the end of their first day on the river, they passed the spot where the Missouri River empties into the Mississippi, at the future site of St. Louis. There, the Missouri's muddy brown water darkens the Mississippi as the waters of the two great rivers mingle.

Meeting the Quapaws

On March 13, they passed the Arkansas River. This was the point Marquette and Jolliet had reached nine years earlier, before turning north. La Salle was not about to turn back before reaching the river's end, however. A few days later, as they paddled through a dense fog, they came upon a group of Native Americans called Quapaws. At first, the explorers feared they would be attacked. But the Quapaws welcomed the newcomers. La Salle visited the Quapaw villages and the two groups got along well. "I cannot tell you the kindness and civility we received," Father Membré wrote about the Quapaws.

Two Quapaws went on with La Salle as guides. Further down the river, they led the explorer to the village of the Taensa people. The Taensa's homes were large and square and arranged in rows, like a European village. "I have never been so surprised," wrote Father Membré.

Marquette and Jolliet sailed partway down the Mississippi River, nine years before La Salle made the trip.

This illustration shows La Salle claiming Louisiana for France.

The French were also astonished by the new kinds of wildlife they encountered. The alligators they found in the river frightened them at first, but soon they were killing the animals for food.

On to the Gulf

As they paddled further down the Mississippi, La Salle knew he was approaching the Gulf of Mexico. The water grew salty. Soon the explorers could feel a stiff sea breeze. Then, on April 9, La Salle saw the Gulf of Mexico stretching out before him. He had become the first European to follow the Mississippi River to its mouth.

La Salle found a bit of dry land on the swampy Gulf Coast and built a monument there. On it was written, "Louis the Great, King of France and Navarre, reigns here." La Salle claimed for King Louis all the lands that the Mississippi River flowed through, as well as all the lands drained by the rivers that led to it. By that simple **proclamation,** La Salle gave France a huge **empire** in North America. He named the land in honor of his king by calling it Louisiana.

EXPLORERS' CLAIMS

When La Salle erected his monument at the mouth of the Mississippi, he was following standard practice for European explorers. When they reached land that was not settled by other European nations, they would often erect some kind of landmark to let others know that the land now belonged to their country. Of course, they did so without considering the Native Americans who already lived on the land. In any case, a nation's claim on land was only as good as its ability to defend it from other nations.

The Return Trip

YOU CAN FOLLOW LA SALLE'S JOURNEY ON THE MAP ON PAGES 42–43.

By reaching the mouth of the Mississippi River, La Salle had earned his place among history's great explorers. He didn't get to savor his achievement for very long, though. He sketched a few hurried maps of the area where the Mississippi empties into the Gulf of Mexico. Then he rushed to return north. It was already April, and La Salle wanted to be sure to arrive back in Québec by November. That was when the last ship for France sailed each year. If news of La Salle's achievement did not make it onto that ship, King Louis would not know of it for another year.

A turn for the worse

Within days of his great triumph, La Salle's luck began to change. As his group headed north, they were attacked by a party of Quinipissas Indians. La Salle's men escaped only after driving the attackers back with **musket** fire. They pushed on north again, but La Salle soon began to feel ill. He became dizzy and developed a fever. Unable to even lift a paddle, La Salle could only sit in a canoe as his men paddled north. Only when they reached the Illinois River did La Salle begin to recover.

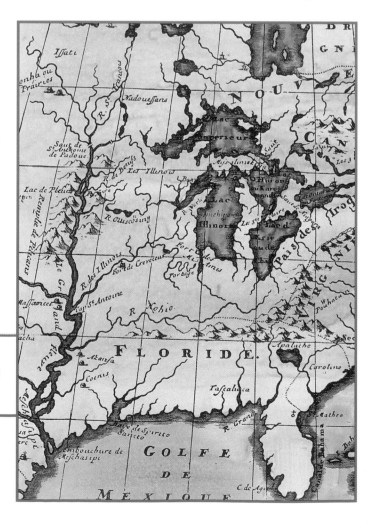

This map of North America, made in the late 1600s, was based on La Salle's trip down the Mississippi River.

32

La Salle's followers feared alligators at first, but soon learned to hunt them for food.

Frontenac departs

There the misfortunes continued. La Salle heard that his friend Frontenac had been removed from the governor's office and ordered back to France. This meant that La Salle had lost his steadiest supporter in New France. Frontenac's replacement was no friend of La Salle's. His name was Le Febvre de La Barre, and he sided with La Salle's enemies and did whatever he could to disrupt La Salle's plans. He even disputed reports of La Salle's great journey. "What is reported of La Salle's discovery seems to me of little use and is larded with lies," he wrote. The new governor seized Fort Frontenac and stopped the shipments of supplies to La Salle. This was fatal to La Salle's plans for a French **empire** along the Mississippi River. There was no way La Salle could build a new line of forts without supplies. Nor could he succeed in his plan with the governor in Québec trying to ruin him. There was only one thing La Salle could do. He would have to return to France and appeal to the government there.

> **In La Salle's words:**
>
> *"I was attacked by a deadly disease, which kept me in danger of my life for forty days."*

Back in France, La Salle found the support he hoped for. The king's ministers reviewed his case and took La Salle's side. They sent a harshly worded letter to La Barre, ordering him to return Fort Frontenac to La Salle and to stop interfering with his plans. Within a year, La Barre was removed from office.

The royal audience

La Salle was pleased, but he had bigger ideas in mind, and he took his plans to the very top. He was granted an **audience** with King Louis XIV and he made the most of it. La Salle told the king that he wanted to return to the mouth of the Mississippi River and establish a **colony** there. He had just claimed the land around the river for the King of France. He now said, "the King's right to the country ... must be safeguarded now that it is formally in his possession." In other words, La Salle thought that the king could keep control of the land by filling it with French people.

La Salle's plan didn't stop there, either. He proposed leading an army of conquest into Spanish lands in Mexico and modern-day Texas. From a base near the Mississippi River, La Salle planned to invade and take control of Spanish territory that was rich in silver.

This illustration shows King Louis XIV's palace at Versailles. The palace was nearing completion when La Salle visited the king.

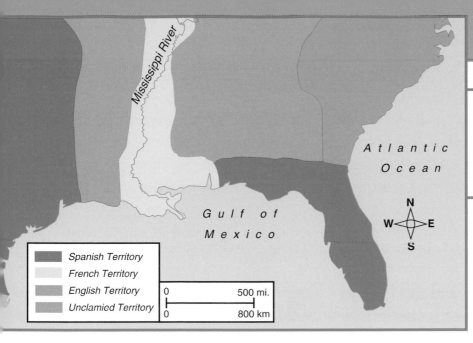

Spanish Territory
French Territory
English Territory
Unclamied Territory

0   500 mi.
0   800 km

This map shows how close the Mississippi River was to Spanish possessions in North America.

This part of the plan especially appealed to the king. He was in favor of any plan that might give France a victory over its Spanish rivals.

The king's blessing

Louis gave La Salle his full support. On April 14, 1684, the king declared that La Salle would "command all the Frenchmen and Indians he may need to execute the orders we have given him." La Salle was given command of 4 ships and 320 people who would follow him to Louisiana. There were families, priests, craft workers, and merchants—enough of them to form a French village in the heart of America. There were also about 100 soldiers and officers. They would form the core of the invasion army. La Salle also planned to recruit thousands of Native Americans to lead into battle.

FRANCE AND SPAIN IN THE NEW WORLD

France and Spain had been bitter rivals for centuries. Gold and silver from the Americas had helped make Spain rich in the 1500s. France was slower to explore and colonize the New World. The two nations fought a series of wars in the 1500s that ended with Spain holding the advantage. However, by the 1680s, France was prepared to compete with Spain for control of land in North America.

La Salle had never led soldiers into battle. He had never commanded a fleet of ships. He had never directed the building of a new colony. Now he was off to do all these things, with the king's blessing.

A Dream Destroyed

YOU CAN FOLLOW LA SALLE'S JOURNEY ON THE MAP ON PAGES 42–43.

La Salle's voyage of 1684 promised to be his most glorious yet. Instead, it was a disaster almost from the very start. He and his fleet of ships left France on July 24, 1684. Within days, the largest ship had to return to port for repairs. There were numerous disagreements between La Salle and the ship's captain, too. Worst of all, La Salle became seriously ill again. After a miserable two-month voyage, his ships arrived at Santo Domingo, a city on the island of Hispaniola in the Caribbean Sea.

Delays and desertion

The entire expedition waited there for La Salle to recover his health. As the weeks passed, many deserted. Finally, La Salle was ready to sail on in search of the mouth of the Mississippi River. On December 28, 1684, he caught sight of the mainland of North America and began looking for the great river. He had no accurate maps to work with, only his own memory of what the river's mouth looked like. Guessing wrong about the river's location, La Salle led his fleet of ships about 400 miles (645 kilometers) west of the Mississippi River. His crew was growing restless and supplies were dwindling, so La Salle decided to go ashore at Matagorda Bay in Texas.

This woodcut shows La Salle's fleet landing in Texas.

Archaeologists have learned a lot from the discovery of La Salle's ship. Most of the hull was intact (right), and they also found some of the cannons (above).

A bad landing

During the landing, the ship holding most of the supplies was torn apart by sharp rocks. Most of their tools, weapons, and food were lost. When La Salle sent one of the ships back east to look for the Mississippi River, the captain simply abandoned La Salle and sailed home to France. La Salle and his colonists tried to make the best of their desperate situation.

Over the next two years, they built a fort along the shore and tried to grow crops. La Salle tried several times to walk east to the Mississippi, but each time he returned to the fort, unsuccessful. The seeds the colonists brought with them from home did not grow well in the coastal soil. One by one, the colonists died from illness, rattlesnake bites, and injuries. In May of 1686, the last of the ships left from La Salle's fleet sank off the coast. La Salle and the others were completely alone, with no way to sail to safety.

THE BELLE

The remains of one of La Salle's ships, the *Belle*, were discovered in Matagorda Bay in 1995. To rescue the contents of the ship, engineers built walls around the ship. The walls formed an enclosure. The engineers then pumped the water out of the enclosure, so that archeologists could reach the ship. They found barrels, guns, cannons, and even rope that had been preserved for more than 300 years.

La Salle's Last Journey

You can follow La Salle's journey on the map on pages 42–43.

Two years after their arrival, only 40 of the 150 colonists who had reached Texas were still alive. With life on the Texas coast becoming more grim every day, La Salle decided he would try one more time to walk to the Mississippi River. He hoped he might find his old friend Tonti there or else somehow make his way back to Canada to get help. La Salle gathered twenty men to accompany him and left the rest of the dwindling **colony** behind to wait for rescue. On January 7, 1687, La Salle began his last journey.

A desperate march

He and his men marched across the prairies of east Texas, struggling to cross rivers and survive violent rainstorms without cover. Two months later, they reached the Trinity River in Texas. They were not yet halfway to the Mississippi River, and their food supply had already run out. La Salle sent a group of men in search of food, while the rest made camp. While they were away, the group searching for food began to argue among themselves. One night, two of them murdered three of the others in their sleep. Then, they decided they would kill La Salle, too.

A statue of La Salle looks out over Matagorda Bay, near the site of his fort.

The death of La Salle

On March 18, La Salle went in search of the group. They had been gone for days, and he feared that they might have become lost. As La Salle neared their camp, the two murderers waited to **ambush** their leader. Hidden behind some tall reeds, they shot at La Salle with **muskets** as he approached. Struck in the head, La Salle fell and died instantly.

Left without their leader, some of La Salle's men fled into the wild, never to be seen again. Incredibly, seven men who stayed loyal to La Salle marched on to the Mississippi River. Eventually, they found Tonti, who after many months helped them return to France. There, they told astonished listeners the tale of La Salle's last days.

This drawing depicts the murder of La Salle by his own men.

In Henri Joutel's words:

Henri Joutel was one of the loyal men who returned to France. He later wrote of his experiences with La Salle.

"His firmness [and] his courage ... would have won at last a glorious success for his grand enterprise, had not all his fine qualities been counterbalanced by ... a harshness towards those under his command, which ... was at last the cause of his death."

La Salle's Legacy

After La Salle's death, Tonti made several attempts to reach the doomed fort on the Texas coast. He never succeeded, however. It wasn't until 1689 that a troop of Spanish soldiers came upon the fort. Inside, they found boxes and barrels that had been destroyed, and old tools that had been left to rust. Outside the fort, on the prairie, they found the remains of three of La Salle's colonists.

The fate of the colonists

Eventually, the Spanish learned that local Native Americans had attacked the fort and overwhelmed the weakened colonists. All were killed, except a few who were adopted by the Indians. So ended La Salle's grand plan to build a French **colony** at the mouth of the Mississippi River. Still, La Salle's vision of a French **empire** that stretched across North America lived on. The vast area in the middle of North American that La Salle claimed for France stayed in French hands for almost a century. In 1699, the French finally did establish a colony at the mouth of the Mississippi. For the next 60 years, the French controlled a **corridor** that ran from Québec on the St. Lawrence River, through the Great Lakes and down the Mississippi to New Orleans. Their forts dotted the shores of these great waterways. This was La Salle's vision, fulfilled only after his death.

This statue of La Salle stands in Chicago's Lincoln Park, not far from the route La Salle traveled to reach the Mississippi River.

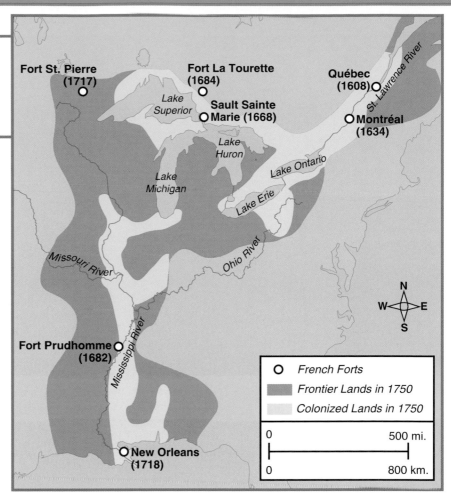

This map shows the extent of French possessions in North America.

Fort St. Pierre (1717)
Fort La Tourette (1684)
Québec (1608)
Lake Superior
Sault Sainte Marie (1668)
Montréal (1634)
Lake Huron
Lake Ontario
Lake Michigan
Lake Erie
St. Lawrence River
Missouri River
Ohio River
Fort Prudhomme (1682)
Mississippi River
New Orleans (1718)

N W E S

○ French Forts
Frontier Lands in 1750
Colonized Lands in 1750

0 — 500 mi.
0 — 800 km.

France's empire

France eventually lost its North American empire to the British and Spanish after a costly war that ended in 1763. In 1800, the French emperor Napoleon regained Louisiana in a secret **treaty** with Spain. He then sold the huge territory to the United States in 1803. The Louisiana Purchase, as it was called, doubled the size of the United States. The name Louisiana lives on as a reminder of the French heritage in North America. So do the many towns and cities with French names along the Mississippi and Illinois Rivers and on the Great Lakes. One of these towns—La Salle, Illinois—is named for the explorer who gave his life to build a French empire in North America.

LA SALLE'S CANNONS

In 1996, a Texas rancher discovered eight old iron cannons buried near the site of La Salle's fort on the Texas coast. Spanish soldiers had buried the cannons after finding the abandoned fort and intended to retrieve them later. They never did, and the cannons lay buried for more than 300 years.

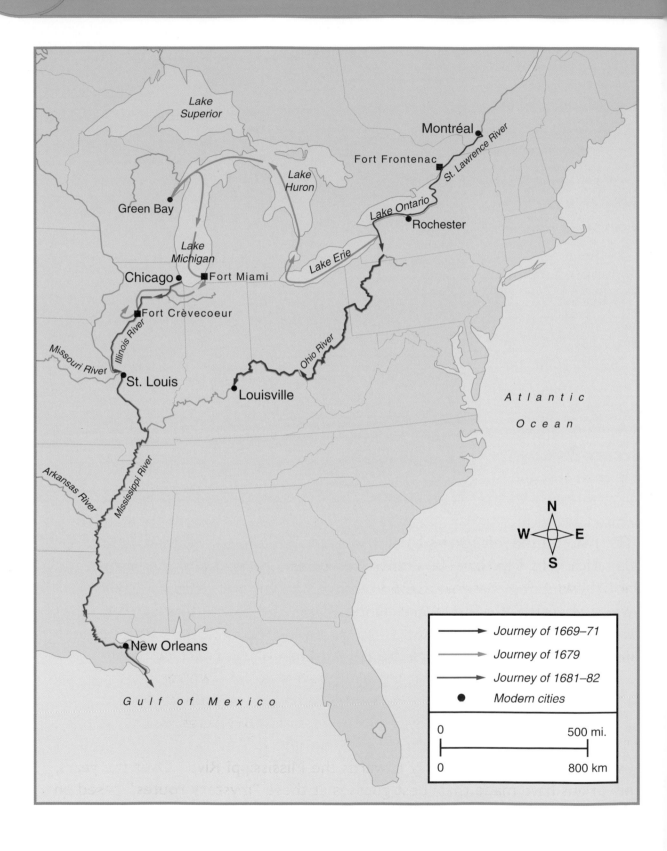

Lake Superior

Montréal

Fort Frontenac

St. Lawrence River

Lake Huron

Green Bay

Lake Ontario

Rochester

Lake Michigan

Lake Erie

Chicago ● ■ Fort Miami

Fort Crèvecoeur

Illinois River

Ohio River

Missouri River

St. Louis

Louisville

Arkansas River

Mississippi River

Atlantic

Ocean

New Orleans

N
W   E
S

Gulf of Mexico

⟶	Journey of 1669–71
⟶	Journey of 1679
⟶	Journey of 1681–82
●	Modern cities

0	500 mi.
0	800 km

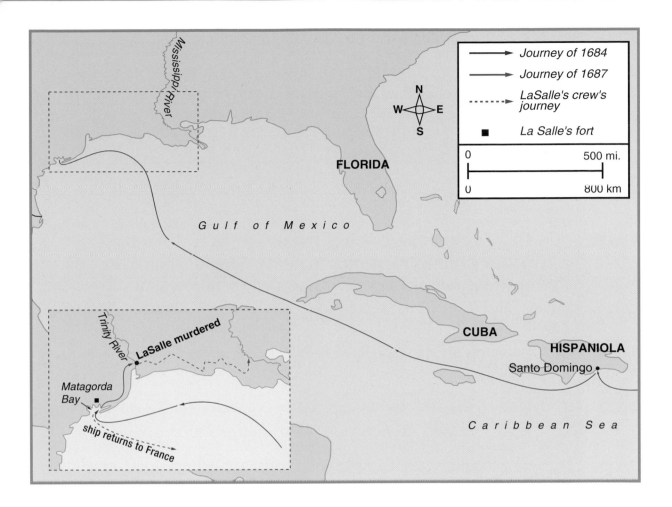

The map on the left shows La Salle's first three voyages of discovery in North America. (His trips back to France to meet with the king and his advisers are not shown.) The journey of 1669–1671, shown in blue, shows La Salle's travels with the group of priests as far as the western shore of Lake Ontario, as well as his continuation of the voyage on his own. Because of the careful records kept by the priests, historians are fairly certain of the route taken on the first part of the journey. However, La Salle's travels on his own remain a mystery, and not everyone agrees on exactly where he went. Historical records give a clear account of La Salle's voyages of 1679 and 1681–82, as well as his trip to Texas in 1684. However, no one is exactly sure of the route he followed overland from Matagorda Bay towards the Mississippi River. Over the years, historians have made their best guesses at these "mystery routes," based on the limited information available.

Timeline

1531	Jacques Cartier explores Canada for France.
1643	René-Robert Cavelier, later known as Sieur de La Salle, is born near Rouen, France and **baptized** on November 22.
1666	Disappointed at not being sent to work overseas, La Salle leaves the **Jesuits.** He sails to New France and settles near Montréal.
1667	Two Seneca come to live on La Salle's land and teach him their language.
1669	La Salle begins his first exploration up the St. Lawrence River with a group of **missionary** priests. Several months later, he splits up with the priests and sets off on his own.
1671	La Salle arrives back in Montréal.
1672	Louis de Buade, Count of Frontenac, is named governor of New France.
1673	Louis Jolliet and Father Jacques Marquette explore the Mississippi River, but they do not travel all the way to its mouth.
	The Iroquois give La Salle and Frontenac permission to build a fort on the shore of Lake Ontario.
1674	La Salle travels to France to meet with government officials and win support for his plans.
1678	King Louis XIV of France gives La Salle permission to build forts along the Mississippi River. La Salle and Henri de Tonti set sail for New France.
1679	La Salle's ship, the *Griffon,* is completed. However, it sinks several months later.
1680	La Salle and his men begin building Fort Crèvecoeur, near present-day Peoria, Illinois.
1682	La Salle travels down the Mississippi River, reaching its mouth at the Gulf of Mexico on April 9.

1684	La Salle departs France to establish a **colony** at the mouth of the Mississippi River.
1686	The last of La Salle's ships sinks, leaving him and the settlers stranded.
1687	La Salle is murdered by his own followers on March 18.
1689	A group of Spanish soldiers discover the remains of La Salle's fort.
1699	France establishes a colony near the mouth of the Mississippi River.
1763	France loses its North American **empire** after war with Spain and England.
1800	France regains its possessions in North America in a secret **treaty** with Spain.
1803	France sells its possessions in North America to the United States in the Louisiana Purchase.
1995	The remains of La Salle's ship, the *Belle,* are discovered in Matagorda Bay, Texas.

More Books to Read

Binns, Tristan Boyer. *Louis Jolliet.* Chicago: Heinemann Library, 2002.

Faber, Harold. *La Salle: Down the Mississippi.* Tarrytown, N.Y.: Marshall Cavendish Corporation, 2002.

Harmon, Daniel E. *Jacques Cartier and the Exploration of Canada.* Broomall, Penn.: Chelsea House Publishers, 2001.

Glossary

ally person or nation that unites with another for a common purpose

ambush to hide in order to attack someone by surprise

astronomy study of the stars and planets

audience opportunity to speak with a king or other high-ranking official

banish to send away from a country or place by the command of authorities

baptize to sprinkle someone with water as part of a ceremony of receiving into the Christian church

blacksmith a person who makes horseshoes and other objects of iron

bluff a cliff or hill with a broad, steep face

cartography science of drawing maps

colony group of people sent out to settle a new territory

confederacy group of people, parties, or states

corridor narrow piece of land that serves as a passageway from one place to another

empire group of territories or people under one ruler

estate fine country house on a large piece of land

export to send or carry goods from one country to another to sell

flatboat a large, flat-bottomed boat used to travel down rivers or other shallow bodies of water

frontier the part of a territory that is at the edge of settlement

griffin mythological creature with the head and wings of an eagle and the body and tail of a lion

gunsmith person who is skilled at making guns

hazard danger or risk

inlet bay or other narrow body of water that runs inland along a shoreline

Jesuit Catholic order founded by Ignatius Loyola in 1534. Jesuits traveled around the world founding missions, trying to convert people to Catholicism.

marshland an area of wet, swampy land

mission place built and run by priests to convert people to a new religion

missionary someone sent to convert people to his or her religion

musket type of gun used from the 1500s to the 1700s

nobleman man born into a class of people with certain social privileges and high social standing

palisade fence made of a series of stakes driven into the ground, used for defense

pelt skin and fur of an animal

portage short route by land either between two bodies of water, or past rapids or other stretches of water too dangerous to sail through

proclamation official public announcement

resource valuable object or the source of valuable objects that can be traded for money or other valuable items

treaty agreement between two or more countries or nations

Index